APR 2 4 2019

LET'S LEARN PRONOUNS!

WE!

BY KATE MIKOLEY

Gareth Stevens
PUBLISHING

Please visit our website, www.garethstevens.com. For a free color catalog of all our high-quality books, call toll free 1-800-542-2595 or fax 1-877-542-2596.

Library of Congress Cataloging-in-Publication Data

Names: Mikoley, Kate author.
Title: Let's learn pronouns! / Kate Mikoley.
Description: New York : Gareth Stevens Publishing, 2019. | Series: Wonderful world of words | Includes bibliographical references and index.
Identifiers: LCCN 2018003840| ISBN 9781538218914 (library bound) | ISBN 9781538218938 (pbk.) | ISBN 9781538218945 (6 pack)
Subjects: LCSH: English language–Pronoun–Juvenile literature.
Classification: LCC PE1261 .M55 2018 | DDC 428.2–dc23
LC record available at https://lccn.loc.gov/2018003840

Published in 2019 by
Gareth Stevens Publishing
111 East 14th Street, Suite 349
New York, NY 10003

Copyright © 2019 Gareth Stevens Publishing

Designer: Katelyn E. Reynolds
Editor: Emily Mahoney

Photo credits: Cover, pp. 1, 19 Monkey Business Images/Shutterstock.com; p. 5 karamysh/Shutterstock.com; p. 7 Stuart Monk/Shutterstock.com; p. 9 VisanuPhotoshop/Shutterstock.com; p. 11 Rawpixel.com/Shutterstock.com; p. 13 wavebreakmedia/Shutterstock.com; p. 15 PR Image Factory/Shutterstock.com; p. 17 TRAIMAK/Shutterstock.com; p. 21 GagliardiImages/Shutterstock.com.

Printed in the United States of America

CPSIA compliance information: Batch #CS18GS: For further information contact Gareth Stevens, New York, New York at 1-800-542-2595.

CONTENTS

Boldface words appear in the glossary.

Replacing Nouns

You may already know that a noun can be a person, place, or thing—like a house. But did you know pronouns are words that can **replace** nouns? Read on to learn more about pronouns. Check your answers on page 22!

You likely already use pronouns every day, even if you don't realize it! Words like *he, she, it, we,* and *they* are all pronouns. *It* is a pronoun that can mean many things. It can be used to talk about your bike, school bus, or favorite stuffed animal.

When using pronouns, make sure it's clear what nouns they're replacing. Say the noun first and replace it with the pronoun later. For example:

"I love riding my bike. It has two wheels."

What word in the second sentence is the pronoun that means "the bike?"

Personal Pronouns

Personal pronouns are pronouns that talk about people. These kinds of pronouns can tell who we're talking about. They can be singular or plural. "Singular" means just one person or thing. "Plural" means more than one person or thing.

He, *she*, *they*, *we*, and *me* are examples of personal pronouns. If you're talking about your sister, you might use the pronoun *she*. This is singular.

What plural pronoun would you use if you are talking about you and your sister?

13

Possessive Pronouns

Some pronouns show possession. Possession means someone has or owns something. *His, her* (or *hers*), and *your* (or *yours*) are examples of possessive pronouns. What pronoun could be used in the following sentence to show the shirt belongs to your mom?

We fold _____ shirt.

15

This and That

This and *that* are often used as pronouns. "This" **usually** means something **nearby**. "That" can mean something far away. Which sentence uses a pronoun to show what color is being talked about?

1. Orange is my favorite color.
2. This is my favorite color.

Don't Repeat Yourself

Pronouns can help us from being too **repetitive**. Look at the following sentences:

The kids went to school. The kids walked to class together.

What pronoun could you replace "the kids" with in the second sentence to stop it from sounding repetitive?

Pronouns All Over

Pronouns are everywhere! For every noun there is also a pronoun that can be used. If you're talking about many apples, you could use the pronouns *they* or *them*. What pronoun would you use if you were talking about just one apple?

GLOSSARY

nearby: not far away; close

personal: belonging to someone

repetitive: saying something again and again

replace: to be used instead of something

usually: when something happens most of the time

ANSWER KEY

22

FOR MORE INFORMATION

BOOKS

Ayers, Linda. *Me, She, He, We: Pronouns Replace Nouns!* North Mankato, MN: Cantata Learning, 2017.

Doyle, Sheri. *What Is a Pronoun?* North Mankato, MN: Capstone Press, 2013.

Murray, Kara. *Nouns and Pronouns.* New York, NY: PowerKids Press, 2014.

WEBSITES

Parts of Speech
www.abcya.com/parts_of_speech.htm
This game will help you learn to spot pronouns and other parts of speech!

The Pronouns
grammaropolis.com/pronoun.php
Find out even more about pronouns here.

Publisher's note to educators and parents: Our editors have carefully reviewed these websites to ensure that they are suitable for students. Many websites change frequently, however, and we cannot guarantee that a site's future contents will continue to meet our high standards of quality and educational value. Be advised that students should be closely supervised whenever they access the internet.

INDEX